The Story of the Good Samaritan

Matthew 22:34–40,
Mark 12:28–31,
and Luke 10:25–37
for children

Written by Teresa Olive • Illustrated by Art Kirchoff

CONCORDIA PUBLISHING HOUSE • SAINT LOUIS

An expert in God's law came down
Where Jesus taught one day,
And asked a question of the Lord
To see what He would say.

"'Love your neighbor
as yourself,'
God tells us in His Word;
But just who *is* my neighbor?"
The lawyer asked the Lord.

The lawyer loved his fellow Jews,
But not Samaritans;
He called them "dogs"
   and would refuse
      To even look at them.

Then Jesus told a story
Of a Jew who had to go
On a journey from Jerusalem
To the town of Jericho.

On the way, some thieves jumped out.
They stripped and beat the man
Till he was bruised and bleeding;
Then they grabbed their loot and ran.

The man lay groaning by the road.
A temple priest walked near.
The man groaned louder, but the priest
Pretended not to hear.

Perhaps the priest thought, *What a shame,*
This man is in distress;
But if I stop to ease his pain,
My robe will be a mess.

Next, a Levite came along—
Who helped the temple priest;
But when he saw the wounded man,
His walking speed increased.

The Levite may have told himself
While scurrying away,
"Surely someone else will stop—
I haven't time today!"

The wounded man grew weaker
As the hours dragged on by;
If someone didn't help
   him soon,
It looked like he would die.

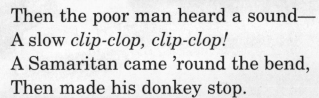

Then the poor man heard a sound—
A slow *clip-clop, clip-clop!*
A Samaritan came 'round the bend,
Then made his donkey stop.

The Samaritan did all he could
To help his "enemy";
He bathed and bandaged
  all his wounds,
    And nursed him tenderly.

When the man was strong enough,
The stranger helped him ride
On the donkey, while he walked
Slowly by its side.

It was getting very late,
When—what a welcome sight!—
They saw a little roadside inn
Where they could spend the night.

The next day the Samaritan
Told the owner of the inn,
"I'll pay you well to nurse this man
Till I come back again."

"Now," Jesus asked the lawyer,
"Of the three, which would you say
Truly was a neighbor
To the man robbed on his way?"

The lawyer said, "The one
      who stopped
And helped to ease his pain."
Then Jesus told the lawyer,
"Now go and do the same!"

We all can be good neighbors
Like the Samaritan that day—
Share God's love with everyone
We meet along the way.

Dear Parents:

God commands us to love our neighbors as ourselves. It is only possible to share that kind of love through the redeeming sacrifice of our Savior, Jesus Christ. His love carried Him to the cross in our place. That's the kind of love, strengthened in us by God's Holy Spirit, that flows from Jesus, through us, and to the people around us.

Explain to your child that God calls us to view anyone who needs our help as a neighbor. We don't have to look hard to find a "wounded" person. They surround us in our family, our neighborhood, our church, our country, our world.

With your child, plan a way to share God's love with a hurting person—invite a lonely friend to dinner and a family devotion, donate food and a picture book about Jesus to your church's welfare cupboard, etc. Pray with your child and ask that the people you help will experience God's love as you share it.

The Editor